Push out the white shapes to make the stencils

Rose

PLATE 1

Push out the white shapes to make the stencils

Daisy

PLATE 3

Tulip

Push out the white shapes to make the stencils

PLATE 5

Push out the white shapes to make the stencils

Iris

PLATE 6

Push out the white shapes to make the stencils

Daffodil

PLATE 8